TABLE

Basic Oven-Baked Potatoes

Baked Potatoes with Caramelized Onions

Baked Potatoes with Mushrooms

Baked Potatoes with Ground Beef

Baked Potatoes with Salmon

Baked Potatoes with Lobster Meat

Baked Potatoes with Crab Meat

Baked Potatoes with Shrimp

Baked Potatoes with Roasted Mushrooms

Baked Potatoes with Roasted Peppers

Baked Potatoes with Broccoli

Baked Potatoes with Brussel Sprouts

Baked Potatoes with Spinach

Baked Potatoes with Potato Salad

Baked Potatoes with Couscous and Chickpeas Salad

Baked Potatoes with Eggplant Salad

BASIC OVEN-BAKED POTATOES
INGREDIENTS

For Potatoes:

2 **Potatoes,** Russet, large

2 Tablespoons **Oil**, olive, virgin

2 teaspoons **Salt,** fine, pink, Himalayan

For Garnish:

Sour cream, grated cheese, butter, green onion, black ground pepper

EQUIPMENT

Small baking tray; wooden skewer; silicone basting brush; kitchen knife.

DIRECTIONS

Step 1: Preheat the oven to 425°F.

Step 2: Wash and towel dry potatoes.

Step 3: Poke the potatoes with a wooden skewer (5-7 times on each potato).

Step 4: Cover potatoes with olive oil using a silicone basting brush.

Step 5: Rub potatoes all over with a generous amount of pink salt.

Step 6: Place coated potatoes onto the baking sheet. Bake for 45 to 55 minutes, depending on the size of potatoes. When potatoes are ready, they will be tender when poked with a wooden skewer.

Serve with sour cream, cheese, butter, cheese, green onion, and black pepper.

Baked Potatoes will keep for three days in a fridge or up to one month in a freezer.

BAKED POTATOES WITH CARAMELIZED ONIONS
INGREDIENTS

For Potatoes:

2 **Potatoes,** Russet, large

2 Tablespoons **Oil**, olive, virgin

2 teaspoons **Salt,** fine, pink, Himalayan

For Stuffing:

2 **Onions**, brown, large

2 Tablespoons **Oil**, olive, virgin

2 Tablespoons **Sugar**, brown

1 teaspoon **Salt,** fine, pink, Himalayan

1 teaspoon Vinegar, balsamic

For Garnish:

Sour cream, grated cheese, butter, green onion, black ground pepper

EQUIPMENT

Small baking tray; medium frying pan; spatula; wooden skewer; silicone basting brush; kitchen knife; measuring cups set.

DIRECTIONS

Make the Baked Potatoes:

Step 1: Preheat the oven to 425°F.

Step 2: Wash and towel dry potatoes.

Step 3: Poke the potatoes with a wooden skewer (5-7 times on each potato).

Step 4: Cover potatoes with olive oil using a silicone basting brush.

Step 5: Rub potatoes all over with a generous amount of pink salt.

Step 6: Place coated potatoes onto the baking sheet. Bake for 45 to 55

minutes, depending on the size of potatoes. When potatoes are ready, they will be tender when poked with a wooden skewer.

Make the Caramelized Onions Stuffing:

You can prepare caramelized onions in advance and heat in the oven, 10-15 minutes before potatoes are ready.

Step 1: Cut the onions in thin half-moons shapes.

Step 2: Heat olive oil in a frying pan. Reduce heat. Place onions into the frying pan. Cook for 10 to 15 minutes over low heat constantly stirring with a spatula. Make sure the onions do not burn.

Step 3: When onions become golden, add brown sugar and balsamic vinegar. Keep frying pan with onions on low heat, occasionally stirring the onions. Onions will start to caramelize. Cook for another 5-7 minutes until onions become thick and brown.

ASSEMBLING

Cut hot baked potato with a knife, remove some of the insides with a fork and place a generous portion of caramelized onions inside.

Serve with sour cream, cheese, butter, cheese, green onion, and black pepper.

Baked Potatoes with Caramelized Onions will keep for two days in a fridge or up to one month in a freezer.

BAKED POTATOES WITH MUSHROOMS
INGREDIENTS

For Potatoes:

2 **Potatoes,** Russet, large

2 Tablespoons **Oil**, olive, virgin

2 teaspoons **Salt,** fine, pink, Himalayan

For Stuffing:

16 Oz **Mushrooms**, white

1 **Onion**, brown, large

2 Tablespoons **Oil**, olive, virgin

1 teaspoon **Salt,** fine, pink, Himalayan

For Garnish:

Sour cream, grated cheese, butter, green onion, black ground pepper

EQUIPMENT

Small baking tray; medium frying pan; spatula; wooden skewer; silicone basting brush; kitchen knife; food scale; measuring cups set.

DIRECTIONS

Make the Baked Potatoes:

Step 1: Preheat the oven to 425°F.

Step 2: Wash and towel dry potatoes.

Step 3: Poke the potatoes with a wooden skewer (5-7 times on each potato)

Step 4: Cover potatoes with olive oil using a silicone basting brush.

Step 5: Rub potatoes all over with a generous amount of pink salt.

Step 6: Place coated potatoes onto the baking sheet. Bake for 45 to 55 minutes, depending on the size of potatoes. When potatoes are ready, they will be tender when poked with a wooden skewer.

Make the Mushroom Stuffing: :

You can prepare mushrooms in advance and heat in the oven, 10-15 minutes before potatoes are ready.

Step 1: Chop the onions into small pieces. Chop the mushrooms into slightly larger ½ inch pieces.

Step 2: Heat olive oil in a frying pan. Reduce heat. Place onions into the frying pan and cook for 5 minutes over low heat constantly stirring with a spatula until they turn golden. Make sure the onions do not burn.

Step 3: When onions become golden, add chopped mushrooms. Keep frying pan with onions and mushrooms on low heat, occasionally stirring. Cook for another 10-15 minutes until mushrooms cook and the excess water evaporates.

ASSEMBLING

Cut hot baked potato with a knife, remove some of the insides with a fork and place a generous portion of mushrooms inside.

Serve with sour cream, cheese, butter, cheese, green onion, and black pepper.

Baked Potatoes with Mushrooms will keep for two days in a fridge or up to one month in a freezer.

Baked Potatoes with Ground Beef

INGREDIENTS

For Potatoes:

2 **Potatoes,** Russet, large

2 Tablespoons **Oil**, olive, virgin

2 teaspoons **Salt,** fine, pink, Himalayan

For Stuffing:

½ Lbs **Ground Beef,** 85% fat

8 Oz **Mushrooms,** white

1 **Onion**, purple, cubed

1 cup **Parsley**, finely chopped, fully packed

1 clove **Garlic**, finely pressed

2 Tablespoons **Oil**, olive, virgin

¼ teaspoon **Salt,** pink, Himalayan

½ teaspoon **Pepper,** black, freshly ground

For Garnish:

Sour cream, grated cheese, butter, green onion, black ground pepper

EQUIPMENT

Small baking tray; medium baking tray; large mixing bowl; spatula; wooden skewer; silicone basting brush; kitchen knife; citrus squeezer; garlic press; paper towel; food scale; measuring cups set.

DIRECTIONS

Make the Baked Potatoes:

Step 1: Preheat the oven to 425°F.

Step 2: Wash and towel dry potatoes.

Step 3: Poke the potatoes with a wooden skewer (5-7 times on each potato).

Step 4: Cover potatoes with olive oil using a silicone basting brush.

Step 5: Rub potatoes all over with a generous amount of pink salt.

Step 6: Place coated potatoes onto the baking sheet. Bake for 45 to 55 minutes, depending on the size of potatoes. When potatoes are ready, they will be tender when poked with a wooden skewer.

Make the Ground Beef Stuffing:

Step 1: Heat up olive oil in a frying pan. Add cubed onion and cook over low-medium heat for 4-5 minutes, constantly stirring, until it turns slightly golden. Add mushrooms and cook for another 15 minutes or until excess water evaporates. Do not cover with the lid.

Add ground beef and cook for another 15-20 minutes. Add pressed garlic, salt, and pepper. Cook for another 3-4 minutes.

ASSEMBLING

Cut hot baked potato with a knife, remove some of the insides with a fork and place a generous portion of ground beef inside. Place and spread one teaspoon of sour cream on top, sprinkle with shredded cheese and bake for 5-7 minutes until cheese melts.

Serve with sour cream, cheese, butter, cheese, green onion, and black pepper.

Baked Potatoes with Ground Beef will keep for two days in a fridge or up to one month in a freezer.

BAKED POTATOES WITH SALMON
INGREDIENTS

For Potatoes:

2 **Potatoes,** Russet, large

2 Tablespoons **Oil**, olive, virgin

2 teaspoons **Salt,** fine, pink, Himalayan

For Stuffing:

¾ Lbs **Salmon,** fillet

1 **Onion**, purple, cubed

8 Oz **Farmers Cheese**

1 cup **Sour cream**

2 Tablespoons **Oil**, olive, virgin

1 cup **Parsley**, finely chopped, loosely packed

1 clove **Garlic**, finely pressed

¼ teaspoon **Salt,** pink, Himalayan

½ teaspoon **Pepper,** black, freshly ground

For Garnish:

Sour cream, grated cheese, butter, green onion, black ground pepper

EQUIPMENT

Small baking tray; medium baking tray; large mixing bowl; spatula; wooden skewer; silicone basting brush; kitchen knife; citrus squeezer; garlic press; paper towel; food scale; measuring cups set.

DIRECTIONS

Make the Baked Potatoes:

Step 1: Preheat the oven to 425°F.

Step 2: Wash and towel dry potatoes.

Step 3: Poke the potatoes with a wooden skewer (5-7 times on each potato).

Step 4: Cover potatoes with olive oil using a silicone basting brush.

Step 5: Rub potatoes all over with a generous amount of pink salt.

Step 6: Place coated potatoes onto the baking sheet. Bake for 45 to 55 minutes, depending on the size of potatoes. When potatoes are ready, they will be tender when poked with a wooden skewer.

Make the Ground Beef Stuffing:

Step 1: Cut salmon on 1-inch cubes. Heat up olive oil in a frying pan. Add cubed onion and cook over low-medium heat for 4-5 minutes, constantly stirring, until it turns slightly golden. Add salmon and cook for 15 minutes until tender. Add salt and pepper. Cook for another 3-4 minutes. Chop cooked salmon with a spatula to create smaller pieces. Set aside to cool.

In a mixing bowl, add cooled salmon, sour cream, farmers cheese, finely chopped parsley, pressed garlic. Slightly mix the ingredients with a spatula to incorporate.

ASSEMBLING

Cut hot baked potato with a knife, remove some of the insides with a fork and place a generous portion of the salmon mixture inside. Place and spread one teaspoon of sour cream on top, sprinkle with shredded cheese and bake for 5-7 minutes until cheese melts.

Serve with sour cream, cheese, butter, cheese, green onion, and black pepper.

Baked Potatoes with Salmon will keep for two days in a fridge or up to one month in a freezer.

Baked Potatoes with Lobster Meat
INGREDIENTS

For Potatoes:

2 **Potatoes,** Russet, large

2 Tablespoons **Oil**, olive, virgin

2 teaspoons **Salt,** fine, pink, Himalayan

For Stuffing:

¾ Lbs **Lobster meat,** frozen

8 Oz **Mushrooms,** white, raw

¼ **Onion**, white, cubed

¾ cup **Sour cream**

2 Tablespoons **Butter**

2 Tablespoons **Oil**, olive, virgin

¼ teaspoon **Salt,** pink, Himalayan

½ teaspoon **Pepper,** black, freshly ground

For Garnish:

Sour cream, grated cheese, butter, green onion, black ground pepper

EQUIPMENT

Small baking tray; medium frying pan; medium heat-proof pot; medium mixing bowl; large mixing bowl, spatula; wooden skewer; silicone basting brush; kitchen knife; citrus squeezer; garlic press; paper towel; food scale; measuring cups set.

DIRECTIONS

Make the Baked Potatoes:

Step 1: Preheat the oven to 425°F.

Step 2: Wash and towel dry potatoes.

Step 3: Poke the potatoes with a wooden skewer (5-7 times on each potato).

Step 4: Cover potatoes with olive oil using a silicone basting brush.

Step 5: Rub potatoes all over with a generous amount of pink salt.

Step 6: Place coated potatoes onto the baking sheet. Bake for 45 to 55 minutes, depending on the size of potatoes. When potatoes are ready, they will be tender when poked with a wooden skewer.

Make the Lobster Stuffing:

Step 1: Place lobster meat in a medium bowl and place onto kitchen counter top to thaw.

Step 2: In a medium pot bring water to boil, add salt, and butter. Place thawed lobster meat into the boiling water. Cook for 4-6 minutes. Drain the water. Set aside to cool.

Step 3: Heat up olive oil in a frying pan. Add cubed onion and cook over low-medium heat for 4-5 minutes, constantly stirring, until it turns slightly golden. Add mushrooms and cook for another 15 minutes or until excess water evaporates. Do not cover with the lid. Set aside to cool.

Step 4: Chop cooked lobster meat into half-inch cubes.

In a large mixing bowl, add cooked lobster meat, sour cream, onion and mushroom mix. Slightly mix the ingredients with a spatula to incorporate.

ASSEMBLING

Cut hot baked potato with a knife, remove some of the insides with a fork and place a generous portion of the lobster mixture inside. Place and spread one teaspoon of sour cream on top, sprinkle with shredded cheese and bake for 5-7 minutes until cheese melts.

Serve with sour cream, cheese, butter, cheese, green onion, and black pepper.

Baked Potatoes with Lobster will keep for two days in a fridge or up to one month in a freezer.

BAKED POTATOES WITH CRAB MEAT
INGREDIENTS

For Potatoes:

2 **Potatoes,** Russet, large

2 Tablespoons **Oil,** olive, virgin

2 teaspoons **Salt,** fine, pink, Himalayan

For Stuffing:

1 Lbs **Crab meat,** frozen

1 **Onion,** white, cubed

¾ cup **Sour cream**

2 Tablespoons **Butter**

2 Tablespoons **Oil,** olive, virgin

¼ teaspoon **Salt,** pink, Himalayan

½ teaspoon **Pepper,** black, freshly ground

For Garnish:

Sour cream, grated cheese, butter, green onion, black ground pepper

EQUIPMENT

Small baking tray; medium frying pan; medium heat-proof pot; medium mixing bowl; large mixing bowl; spatula; wooden skewer; silicone basting brush; kitchen knife; citrus squeezer; garlic press; paper towel; food scale; measuring cups set.

DIRECTIONS

Make the Baked Potatoes:

Step 1: Preheat the oven to 425°F.

Step 2: Wash and towel dry potatoes.

Step 3: Poke the potatoes with a wooden skewer (5-7 times on each potato)

Step 4: Cover potatoes with olive oil using a silicone basting brush.

Step 5: Rub potatoes all over with a generous amount of pink salt.

Step 6: Place coated potatoes onto the baking sheet. Bake for 45 to 55 minutes, depending on the size of potatoes. When potatoes are ready, they will be tender when poked with a wooden skewer.

Make the Crab Stuffing:

Step 1: Place crab meat in a medium bowl and place onto kitchen counter top to thaw.

Step 2: In a medium pot bring water to boil, add salt, and butter. Place thawed crab meat into the boiling water. Cook for 4-6 minutes. Drain the water. Set aside to cool.

Step 3: Heat up olive oil in a frying pan. Add cubed onion and cook over low-medium heat for 4-5 minutes, constantly stirring, until it turns slightly golden. Set In a medium pot bring water to boil, add salt, and butter. Place thawed crab meat into the boiling water. Cook for 4-6 minutes. Drain the water. Set aside to cool.

Step 4: Chop cooked crab meat into half-inch cubes.

In a large mixing bowl, add cooked crab meat, sour cream, and onion. Slightly mix the ingredients with a spatula to incorporate.

ASSEMBLING

Cut hot baked potato with a knife, remove some of the insides with a fork and place a generous portion of crab mixture inside. Place and spread one teaspoon of sour cream on top, sprinkle with shredded cheese and bake for 5-7 minutes until cheese melts.

Serve with sour cream, cheese, butter, cheese, green onion, and black pepper.

Baked Potatoes with Crab meat will keep for two days in a fridge or up to one month in a freezer.

BAKED POTATOES WITH SHRIMP
INGREDIENTS

For Potatoes:

2 **Potatoes,** Russet, large

2 Tablespoons **Oil**, olive, virgin

2 teaspoons **Salt,** fine, pink, Himalayan

For Stuffing:

1 Lbs **Shrimps,** peeled, without tails

1 **Onion**, white, cubed

¾ cup **Sour cream**

2 Tablespoons **Butter**

2 Tablespoons **Oil**, olive, virgin

¼ teaspoon **Salt,** pink, Himalayan

½ teaspoon **Pepper,** black, freshly ground

For Garnish:

Sour cream, grated cheese, butter, green onion, black ground pepper.

EQUIPMENT

Small baking tray; medium frying pan; medium heat-proof pot; medium mixing bowl; large mixing bowl; spatula; wooden skewer; silicone basting brush; kitchen knife; citrus squeezer; garlic press; paper towel; food scale; measuring cups set.

DIRECTIONS

Make the Baked Potatoes:

Step 1: Preheat the oven to 425°F.

Step 2: Wash and towel dry potatoes.

Step 3: Poke the potatoes with a wooden skewer (5-7 times on each potato).

Step 4: Cover potatoes with olive oil using a silicone basting brush.

Step 5: Rub potatoes all over with a generous amount of pink salt.

Step 6: Place coated potatoes onto the baking sheet. Bake for 45 to 55 minutes, depending on the size of potatoes. When potatoes are ready, they will be tender when poked with a wooden skewer.

Make the Shrimp Stuffing:

Step 1: If shrimps are frozen, place shrimps in a medium bowl and place onto kitchen counter top to thaw.

Step 2: In a medium pot bring water to boil, add salt, and butter. Place thawed shrimps into the boiling water. Cook for 4-5 minutes. Drain the water. Set aside to cool.

Step 3: Heat up olive oil in a frying pan. Add cubed onion and cook over low-medium heat for 4-5 minutes, constantly stirring, until it turns slightly golden. Set aside to cool.

Step 4: Chop cooked shrimps into half inch cubes.

In a large mixing bowl, add chopped shrimps, sour cream, and onion. Slightly mix the ingredients with a spatula to incorporate. Set aside.

ASSEMBLING

Cut hot baked potato with a knife, remove some of the insides with a fork. Set it aside.

Add the potatoes insides into the shrimp mixture and incorporate evenly with a spatula.

Place a generous portion of shrimp mixture inside of each potato. Place and spread one teaspoon of sour cream on top, sprinkle with shredded cheese and bake for 5-7 minutes until cheese melts.

Serve with sour cream, cheese, butter, cheese, green onion, and black pepper.

Baked Potatoes with Crab meat will keep for two days in a fridge or up to one month in a freezer.

BAKED POTATOES WITH ROASTED MUSHROOMS

INGREDIENTS

For Potatoes:

2 **Potatoes,** Russet, large

2 Tablespoons **Oil**, olive, virgin

2 teaspoons **Salt,** fine, pink, Himalayan

For Stuffing:

16 Oz **Mushrooms**, white

1 **Onion**, brown, large

2 Tablespoons **Oil**, olive, virgin

1 teaspoon **Salt,** fine, pink, Himalayan

For Garnish:

Sour cream, grated cheese, butter, green onion, black ground pepper

EQUIPMENT

Small baking tray; medium frying pan; spatula; wooden skewer; silicone basting brush; kitchen knife; food scale; measuring cups set.

DIRECTIONS

Make the Baked Potatoes:

Step 1: Preheat the oven to 425°F.

Step 2: Wash and towel dry potatoes.

Step 3: Poke the potatoes with a wooden skewer (5-7 times on each potato).

Step 4: Cover potatoes with olive oil using a silicone basting brush.

Step 5: Rub potatoes all over with a generous amount of pink salt.

Step 6: Place coated potatoes onto the baking sheet. Bake for 45 to 55 minutes, depending on the size of potatoes. When potatoes are ready, they will be tender when poked with a wooden skewer.

Make the Mushroom Stuffing:

You can prepare mushrooms in advance and heat in the oven, 10-15 minutes before potatoes are ready.

Step 1: Chop the onions into small pieces. Chop the mushrooms into slightly larger ½ inch pieces.

Step 2: Preheat oven to 425°F. Place mushrooms and onions on a baking tray and brush them with vegetable oil using a silicone basting brush.

Roast for about 15-20 minutes.

ASSEMBLING

Cut hot baked potato with a knife, remove some of the insides with a fork and place a generous portion of mushrooms inside.

Serve with sour cream, cheese, butter, cheese, green onion, and black pepper.

Baked Potatoes with Mushrooms will keep for two days in a fridge or up to one month in a freezer.

Baked Potatoes with Roasted Peppers

INGREDIENTS

For Potatoes:

2 **Potatoes,** Russet, large

2 Tablespoons **Oil**, olive, virgin

2 teaspoons **Salt,** fine, pink, Himalayan

For Stuffing:

4 **Bell Peppers**, red, large

1 **Onions**, brown, large

2 Tablespoons **Oil**, olive, virgin

2 Teaspoons **Sour cream**, full fat

1 cup **Cheese**, shredded, Italian blend

1 ½ teaspoon **Salt,** fine, pink, Himalayan

½ teaspoon **Paprika,** ground

Black Ground Pepper, to taste

For Garnish:

Sour cream, grated cheese, butter, green onion, black ground pepper

EQUIPMENT

Small baking tray; spatula; wooden skewer; silicone basting brush; kitchen knife; measuring cups set.

DIRECTIONS

Make the Baked Potatoes:

Step 1: Preheat the oven to 425°F.

Step 2: Wash and towel dry potatoes.

Step 3: Poke the potatoes with a wooden skewer (5-7 times on each potato)

Step 4: Cover potatoes with olive oil using a silicone basting brush.

Step 5: Rub potatoes all over with a generous amount of pink salt.

Step 6: Place coated potatoes onto the baking sheet. Bake for 45 to 55 minutes, depending on the size of potatoes. When potatoes are ready, they will be tender when poked with a wooden skewer.

Make the Red Pepper Stuffing:

You can prepare peppers in advance and heat up in the oven, 10-15 minutes before potatoes are ready.

Step 1: Chop the onions into small pieces. Chop the red peppers into small pieces.

Step 2: Preheat oven to 425°F. Place peppers and onions on a baking tray and brush them with vegetable oil using a silicone basting brush. Sprinkle with salt, paprika, and ground black pepper.

Roast for about 25 – 30 minutes.

ASSEMBLING

Cut hot baked potato with a knife, remove some of the insides with a fork and place a generous portion of red peppers inside. Place and spread one teaspoon of sour cream on top, sprinkle with shredded cheese and bake for 5-7 minutes until cheese melts.

Serve with sour cream, cheese, butter, cheese, green onion, and black pepper.

Baked Potatoes with Red peppers will keep for two days in a fridge or up to one month in a freezer.

Baked Potatoes with Broccoli
INGREDIENTS

For Potatoes:

2 **Potatoes,** Russet, large

2 Tablespoons **Oil**, olive, virgin

2 teaspoons **Salt,** fine, pink, Himalayan

For Stuffing:

1 Head, **Broccoli,** separated on florets

1 **Onion**, brown, large

1 Tablespoons **Oil**, olive, virgin

¾ cup **Sour cream**, full fat

½ cup **Farmers cheese**

½ and ½ cup **Cheese**, shredded, Italian blend

1 ½ teaspoon **Salt,** fine, pink, Himalayan

½ teaspoon **Garlic,** powder

Black Ground Pepper, to taste

For Garnish:

Sour cream, grated cheese, butter, green onion, black ground pepper

EQUIPMENT

Small baking dish; small baking tray; small mixing bowl; spatula; wooden skewer; silicone basting brush; kitchen knife; measuring cups set.

DIRECTIONS

Make the Baked Potatoes:

Step 1: Preheat the oven to 425°F.

Step 2: Wash and towel dry potatoes.

Step 3: Poke the potatoes with a wooden skewer (5-7 times on each potato)

Step 4: Cover potatoes with olive oil using a silicone basting brush.

Step 5: Rub potatoes all over with a generous amount of pink salt.

Step 6: Place coated potatoes onto the baking sheet. Bake for 45 to 55 minutes, depending on the size of potatoes. When potatoes are ready, they will be tender when poked with a wooden skewer.

Make the Broccoli Stuffing:

You can prepare broccoli in advance and heat up in the oven, 10-15 minutes before potatoes are ready.

Step 1: Chop the onions into small pieces. Chop the broccoli florets into small pieces.

Step 2: Preheat oven to 425°F.

In a small mixing bowl combine broccoli florets, onions, sour cream, olive oil, farmers cheese, garlic powder, ground pepper, and salt. Mix well to combine.

Place broccoli mixture into a baking tray.

Bake for about 30 – 35 minutes.

ASSEMBLING

Cut hot baked potato with a knife, remove some of the insides with a fork and place a generous portion of baked broccoli inside. Place and spread one teaspoon of sour cream on top, sprinkle with shredded cheese and bake for 5-7 minutes until cheese melts.

Serve with sour cream, cheese, butter, cheese, green onion, and black pepper.

Baked Potatoes with Broccoli will keep for two days in a fridge or up to one month in a freezer.

BAKED POTATOES WITH BRUSSEL SPROUTS

INGREDIENTS

For Potatoes:

2 **Potatoes,** Russet, large

2 Tablespoons **Oil**, olive, virgin

2 teaspoons **Salt,** fine, pink, Himalayan

For Stuffing:

16 **Brussel Sprouts**, raw

1 **Onion**, brown, large

1 Tablespoons **Oil**, olive, virgin

¾ cup **Sour cream**, full fat

½ cup **Farmers cheese**

½ and ½ cup **Cheese**, shredded, Italian blend

1 ½ teaspoon **Salt,** fine, pink, Himalayan

½ teaspoon **Garlic,** powder

Black Ground Pepper, to taste

For Garnish:

Sour cream, grated cheese, butter, green onion, black ground pepper

EQUIPMENT

Small baking dish; small baking tray; small mixing bowl; spatula; wooden skewer; silicone basting brush; kitchen knife; measuring cups set.

DIRECTIONS

Make the Baked Potatoes:

Step 1: Preheat the oven to 425°F.

Step 2: Wash and towel dry potatoes.

Step 3: Poke the potatoes with a wooden skewer (5-7 times on each potato).

Step 4: Cover potatoes with olive oil using a silicone basting brush.

Step 5: Rub potatoes all over with a generous amount of pink salt.

Step 6: Place coated potatoes onto the baking sheet. Bake for 45 to 55 minutes, depending on the size of potatoes. When potatoes are ready, they will be tender when poked with a wooden skewer.

Make the Brussel Sprouts Stuffing:

You can prepare Brussel sprouts in advance and heat up in the oven, 10-15 minutes before potatoes are ready.

Step 1: Chop the onions into small pieces. Cut each of the Brussel sprouts into quarters.

Step 2: Preheat oven to 425°F.

In a small mixing bowl combine Brussel sprouts, onions, sour cream, olive oil, farmers cheese, garlic powder, ground pepper, and salt. Mix well to combine.

Place Brussel sprouts mixture into a baking tray.

Bake for about 30 – 35 minutes.

ASSEMBLING

Cut hot baked potato with a knife, remove some of the insides with a fork and place a generous portion of baked Brussel sprouts inside. Place and spread one teaspoon of sour cream on top, sprinkle with shredded cheese and bake for 5-7 minutes until cheese melts.

Serve with sour cream, cheese, butter, cheese, green onion, and black pepper.

Baked Potatoes with Brussel sprouts will keep for two days in a fridge or up to one month in a freezer.

BAKED POTATOES WITH SPINACH

INGREDIENTS

For Potatoes:

2 **Potatoes,** Russet, large

2 Tablespoons **Oil**, olive, virgin

2 teaspoons **Salt,** fine, pink, Himalayan

For Stuffing:

16 Oz **Spinach,** raw

1 **Onion**, brown, large

1 Tablespoons **Oil**, olive, virgin

½ cup **Sour cream**, full fat

¾ cup **Farmers cheese**

½ and ½ cup **Cheese**, shredded, Italian blend

1 ½ teaspoon **Salt,** fine, pink, Himalayan

½ teaspoon **Paprika,** powder

½ teaspoon **Garlic,** powder

Black Ground Pepper, to taste

For Garnish:

Sour cream, grated cheese, butter, green onion, black ground pepper

EQUIPMENT

Small baking dish; small baking tray; small mixing bowl; spatula; wooden skewer; silicone basting brush; kitchen knife; food scale; measuring cups set.

DIRECTIONS

Make the Baked Potatoes:

Step 1: Preheat the oven to 425°F.

Step 2: Wash and towel dry potatoes.

Step 3: Poke the potatoes with a wooden skewer (5-7 times on each potato)

Step 4: Cover potatoes with olive oil using a silicone basting brush.

Step 5: Rub potatoes all over with a generous amount of pink salt.

Step 6: Place coated potatoes onto the baking sheet. Bake for 45 to 55 minutes, depending on the size of potatoes. When potatoes are ready, they will be tender when poked with a wooden skewer.

Make the Spinach Stuffing:

You can prepare spinach in advance and heat up in the oven, 10-15 minutes before potatoes are ready.

Step 1: Chop the onions into small pieces. Chop spinach.

Step 2: Preheat oven to 425°F.

In a small mixing bowl combine spinach, onions, sour cream, olive oil, farmers cheese, garlic powder, paprika, ground pepper, and salt. Mix well to combine.

Place spinach mixture into a baking tray.

Bake for about 30 – 35 minutes.

ASSEMBLING

Cut hot baked potato with a knife, remove some of the insides with a fork and place a generous portion of baked spinach inside. Place and spread one teaspoon of sour cream on top, sprinkle with shredded cheese and bake for 5-7 minutes until cheese melts.

Serve with sour cream, cheese, butter, cheese, green onion, and black pepper.

Baked Potatoes with Brussel sprouts will keep for two days in a fridge or up to one month in a freezer.

BAKED POTATOES WITH POTATO SALAD
INGREDIENTS

For Potatoes:

2 **Potatoes,** Russet, large

2 Tablespoons **Oil**, olive, virgin

2 teaspoons **Salt,** fine, pink, Himalayan

For Stuffing:

1 ½ Lbs. **Baby Potatoes**, golden, cut in thin rings

¾ Lbs. **Carrots**, peeled, cut in thin rings

1 **Cucumber**, medium, finely cut

1 **Onion**, purple, thinly sliced

1 cup **Dill,** chopped

½ cup **Parsley**, finely chopped, fully packed

¾ cup **Capers**

½ plus ½ **Lemon**, large, juice of

½ **Lime**, large, juice of

3 cloves **Garlic**, finely pressed

4 tablespoons **Oil**, olive, extra-virgin

4 tablespoons **Oil,** coconut, extra-virgin

2 tablespoons **Vinegar,** white

¼ teaspoon **Salt,** pink, Himalayan

½ teaspoon **Pepper,** black, freshly ground

½ teaspoon **Oregano,** dried

For Garnish:

Sour cream, grated cheese, butter, green onion, black ground pepper.

EQUIPMENT

Small baking tray; medium baking tray, large mixing bowl; spatula; wooden skewer; silicone basting brush; kitchen knife; citrus squeezer; garlic press; paper towel; food scale; measuring cups set.

DIRECTIONS

Make the Baked Potatoes:

Step 1: Preheat the oven to 425°F.

Step 2: Wash and towel dry potatoes.

Step 3: Poke the potatoes with a wooden skewer (5-7 times on each potato).

Step 4: Cover potatoes with olive oil using a silicone basting brush.

Step 5: Rub potatoes all over with a generous amount of pink salt.

Step 6: Place coated potatoes onto the baking sheet. Bake for 45 to 55 minutes, depending on the size of potatoes. When potatoes are ready, they will be tender when poked with a wooden skewer.

Make the Potato Salad Stuffing:

Step 1: Cut the potatoes and carrots into small cubes. Place them on a baking tray, sprinkle with pressed garlic, salt, and pepper. Brush vegetables with coconut oil using a silicone basting brush. *If the coconut oil is too firm, liquify it by putting it on a water bath and heat it up until it melts and becomes liquid.*

Roast for 40-50 minutes or until ready when it is easily pierced with a fork or a skewer. Set aside to cool for a few minutes. Transfer onto a paper towel to dry.

Step 2: In a large mixing bowl combine vegetables, herbs, and capers.

Step 3: Squeeze one half of a lemon with the citrus squeezer into a small mixing bowl. Add finely cut onion rings. Set aside for one hour to marinate, then add into the salad.

Step 4: Squeeze ½ of lime and ½ of lemon with the citrus squeezer into a cup. Pour the juice on top of the salad. Add salt and pepper, and olive oil.

Toss to incorporate.

ASSEMBLING

Cut hot baked potato with a knife, remove some of the insides with a fork and place a generous portion of potato salad inside. Place and spread one teaspoon of sour cream on top, sprinkle with shredded cheese and bake for 5-7 minutes until cheese melts.

Serve with sour cream, cheese, butter, cheese, green onion, and black pepper.

Baked Potatoes with Potato Salad will keep for two days in a fridge or up to one month in a freezer.

Baked Potatoes with Couscous and Chickpeas Salad

INGREDIENTS

For Potatoes:

2 **Potatoes,** Russet, large

2 Tablespoons **Oil,** olive, virgin

2 teaspoons **Salt,** fine, pink, Himalayan

For Stuffing:

1 15 Oz can **Chickpeas**, drained and rinsed

2 cups **Couscous,** pearl

2 cups **Grape Tomatoes**, quartered

2 **Cucumbers**, medium, finely chopped

¾ cup **Olives**, Kalamata, pitted

1 cup **Green onions**, finely chopped, fully packed

1 cup **Cilantro**, finely chopped, fully packed

½ cup **Dill,** chopped

½ cup **Basil,** chopped

½ **Lime**, large, juice of

½ **Lemon**, large, juice of

4 tablespoons **Oil,** olive, extra-virgin

¼ teaspoon **Salt,** pink, Himalayan

½ teaspoon **Pepper,** black, freshly ground

For Garnish:

Sour cream, grated cheese, butter, green onion, black ground pepper

EQUIPMENT

Small baking tray; heat-proof bowl; large mixing bowl; spatula; wooden

skewer; silicone basting brush; kitchen knife; citrus squeezer; garlic press; paper towel; food scale; measuring cups set.

DIRECTIONS

Make the Baked Potatoes:

Step 1: Preheat the oven to 425°F.

Step 2: Wash and towel dry potatoes.

Step 3: Poke the potatoes with a wooden skewer (5-7 times on each potato).

Step 4: Cover potatoes with olive oil using a silicone basting brush.

Step 5: Rub potatoes all over with a generous amount of pink salt.

Step 6: Place coated potatoes onto the baking sheet. Bake for 45 to 55 minutes, depending on the size of potatoes. When potatoes are ready, they will be tender when poked with a wooden skewer.

Make the Couscous and Chickpeas Salad Stuffing:

Step 1: In a heat-proof bowl add three cups of water. Bring it to boil. Add couscous to boiling water, cover and cook for 5-10 minutes. Once ready, drain the water and set aside to cool.

Step 2: In a large mixing bowl combine vegetables and herbs. Add cooled couscous. Drain water from canned chickpeas. Add chickpeas.

Step 3. Squeeze lime and lemon with the citrus squeezer into a cup. Pour the juice on top of the salad. Add salt and pepper, and olive oil. Toss to incorporate.

ASSEMBLING

Cut hot baked potato with a knife, remove some of the insides with a fork and place a generous portion of the chickpeas salad inside. Place and spread one teaspoon of sour cream on top, sprinkle with shredded cheese and bake for 5-7 minutes until cheese melts.

Serve with sour cream, cheese, butter, cheese, green onion, and black pepper.

Baked Potatoes with Chickpeas Salad will keep for two days in a fridge or up to one month in a freezer.

Baked Potatoes with Eggplant Salad

INGREDIENTS

For Potatoes:

2 **Potatoes,** Russet, large

2 Tablespoons **Oil**, olive, virgin

2 teaspoons **Salt,** fine, pink, Himalayan

For Stuffing:

1 15 Oz can **Chickpeas**, drained and rinsed

1 **Eggplant**, large, thinly sliced

4 **Tomatoes**, finely cut

1 **Cucumber**, medium, finely cut

1 **Onion**, purple, thinly sliced

1 cup **Parsley**, finely chopped, fully packed

1 cup **Dill,** chopped

½ cup **Basil,** chopped

1 plus ½ **Lemon**, large, juice of

½ **Lime**, large, juice of

1 clove **Garlic**, finely pressed

4 tablespoons **Oil,** olive, extra-virgin

4 tablespoons **Oil,** coconut, extra-virgin

¼ teaspoon **Salt,** pink, Himalayan

½ teaspoon **Pepper,** black, freshly ground

For Garnish:

Sour cream, grated cheese, butter, green onion, black ground pepper.

EQUIPMENT

Small baking tray; large mixing bowl; spatula; wooden skewer; silicone basting brush; kitchen knife; citrus squeezer; garlic press; paper towel; food scale; measuring cups set.

DIRECTIONS

Make the Baked Potatoes:

Step 1: Preheat the oven to 425°F.

Step 2: Wash and towel dry potatoes.

Step 3: Poke the potatoes with a wooden skewer (5-7 times on each potato).

Step 4: Cover potatoes with olive oil using a silicone basting brush.

Step 5: Rub potatoes all over with a generous amount of pink salt.

Step 6: Place coated potatoes onto the baking sheet. Bake for 45 to 55 minutes, depending on the size of potatoes. When potatoes are ready, they will be tender when poked with a wooden skewer.

Make the Couscous and Eggplant Salad Stuffing:

Step 1: Preheat oven to 425°F. Cut the eggplant into small cubes. Place them onto a baking tray, sprinkle with pressed garlic, salt and pepper, and brush with coconut oil using a silicone basting brush. *If the coconut oil is too firm, liquify it by putting it on a water bath and heat it up until it melts and becomes liquid.*

Roast for 35 minutes or until ready when it is easily pierced with a fork or a skewer. Set aside to cool for a few minutes. Transfer onto a paper towel to dry.

Step 2: In a large mixing bowl combine vegetables and herbs. Drain water from canned chickpeas. Add chickpeas.

Step 3. Squeeze one lemon with the citrus squeezer into a small mixing bowl. Add finely cut onion rings. Set aside for one hour to marinate. Then add into the salad.

Step 4. Squeeze ½ of lime and ½ of lemon with the citrus squeezer into a cup. Pour the juice on top of the salad. Add salt and pepper, and olive oil.

Printed in the USA
CPSIA information can be obtained
at www.ICGtesting.com
LVHW040012311024
795306LV00033B/489